FIGURE TEMPLATES FOR FASHION ILLUSTRATION

OVER 150 TEMPLATES FOR FASHION DESIGN

Patrick John Ireland

Batsford

Acknowledgements

Photograph by Rainer Usselmann

Patrick John Ireland is a member of Britain's Chartered Society of Designers. He is a Fashion Designer and Illustrator, and Lecturer organising Fashion Workshops for students and lecturers of fashion, and has also been a visiting lecturer at colleges throughout the country including The London College of Fashion, The London Institute, Cordwainers College London, The Art Institute at Bournemouth, Berkshire College of Art and Brunel University. He is also the author of several previous books for Batsford.

Acknowledgements

I would like to extend my thanks to Thelma Nye, Theresa Colburn and Christina Barry for their advice and support, and all the students and lecturers in the many colleges and workshops I have worked with for their encouragement in producing this book, thanks also to Simon Rosenheim and Wladek Szechter at Batsford who designed the book.

ISBN 0 7134 8572 8

Printed in Spain

Volume © B T Batsford 2000

First published in 2000
Reprinted 2002, 2003, 2004
B T Batsford
The Chrysalis Building
Bramley Road
London W10 6SP
www.batsford.com

An imprint of Chrysalis Books Group plc

Distributed in the United States and Canada by Sterling Publishing Co., 387 Park Avenue South, New York, NY10016, USA

Contents

Introduction

The aim of this book is to help students to develop design sketching and presentation skills.

Initially many students of design find it difficult to sketch the figure and express ideas onto paper. If you should have difficulty drawing the figure for fashion design, the methods illustrated will be helpful in developing your fashion design drawing skills in the early stages.

The book explains the use of the figure templates and simple methods of developing figure poses as an aid to expressing your ideas.

The template enables you to sketch and design in a free style over the impression of the figure with the use of semi-transparent layout paper or a light box. The figure should not be traced, only used as a quick guide sketching freely over the impression through the paper.

The basic figure proportions are illustrated from 7-$7^{1}/_{2}$ head measurements to the more exaggerated figures often used in fashion drawing to convey a strong fashion image. The proportions vary from 8-9 and 10 head measurements into the figure.

Students of fashion courses rely on their design drawing and presentation work for assessments, competitions and interviews as examples of work for a portfolio.

It is very important for the student to be aware of the different areas of fashion drawing and the illustrative skills that best suit the purpose of the drawing.

The student is required to produce sketch books and research work when developing a design theme and design development sheets exploring ideas for a collection. The final stage would be the presentation sheets and boards together with working drawings often referred to as Flats.

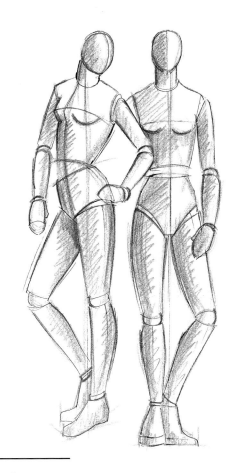

Stage 1

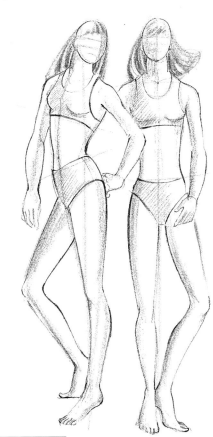

Stage 2

✔ The book explains how to develop your own figure poses working from a model, photographs or constructing figures from imagination.

✔ It is divided into three sections Women, Men and Children providing a selection of Figure Templates: Front, Back and Side views in different poses from standing, moving and action poses.

✔ The different measurements are illustrated from the basic average proportions to the very extreme with information on illustrative techniques, layout and presentation effects.

✔ The figures may be copied, traced, photocopied, scanned into a computer, and enlarged to the size you require or used as a guide for producing templates.

✔ Most fashion design courses provide periods of Life Drawing and Costume Life. It is important to develop our drawing skills with observation and practise. However, if in the early stages you have difficulty expressing your design ideas onto paper you will find the following methods helpful.

✔ When designing, the template is a tool which enables the designer to express design ideas quickly and accurately onto the paper (or computer).

✔ It may not always be necessary to use the figure template, but, given time and confidence with practise and an awareness of the form beneath the clothing, it will become possible to create the design sketch.

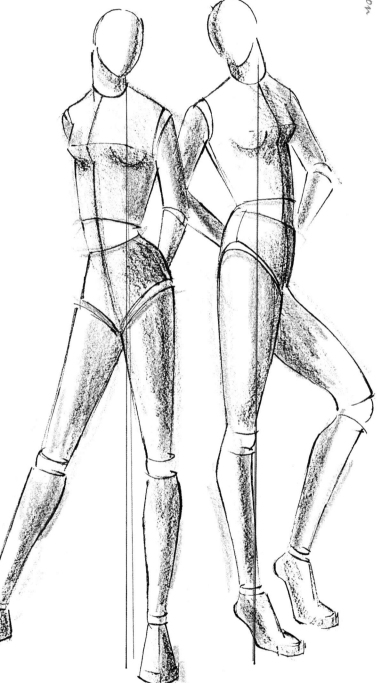

Figures developed from the basic forms

The Clothed Figure

When sketching a fashion design of the clothed figure, consider the solid form of the body beneath the clothing. Simply suggesting surface effects will not necessarily produce the required effect for a fashion sketch.

The areas where the body supports the clothing can suggest the characteristics and behaviour of the material.

Certain fabrics and their characteristics influence the way in which the form of the figure is revealed. Heavy stiff fabrics, i.e. tweeds or linen, tend to drape and fold in an angular way, producing hard folds resisting movement.

Soft fabrics such as jersey or silk hang and drape in soft folds and show the form of the figure more clearly.

Designs which are cut loosely, though not close to the shape of the figure, can still reveal the figure in parts, when the skirt drapes over the legs in movement or a sleeve drapes over the arm.

Sketch book: Make observational drawings of the figure in movement, observing the characteristics of different fabrics and the way in which they fall and drape round the figure. This will help when sketching from memory.

Soft folds

Hard folds

Proportions

When producing fashion sketches and presentation drawings it is important to be aware of the standard proportions of the human figure. One of the most effective methods of classification is the number of times the length of the head fits into the total height of the body.

✔ Proportions vary from person to person. The classical Greek and Renaissance figures were eight heads in height, the head being the unit of measure.

✔ Fashion illustrators and designers often elongate figures nine or more head lengths to project a fashion image.

✔ In nature, the average height of the human body is $7\frac{1}{2}$ heads. However, for fashion the eight to nine head figure is more elegant and fashionable.

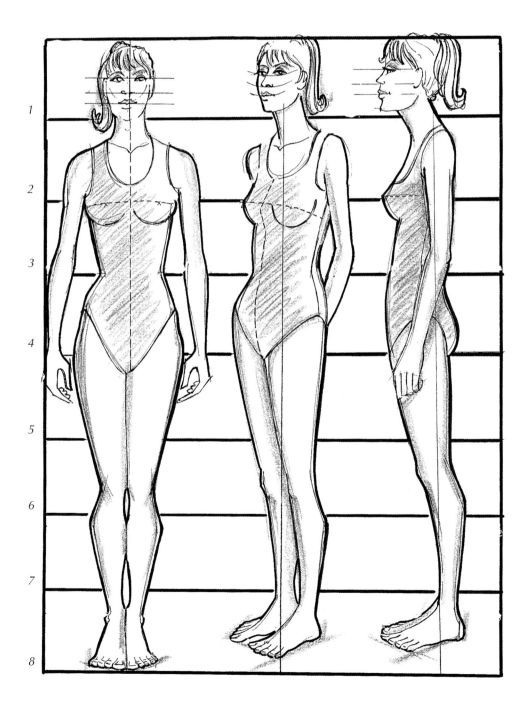

✔ If you stylise or caricature the fashion drawing to illustrate a particular image this may be achieved by simply increasing the height of the figure to nine or ten measurements of the head into the body. However, any departure from the eight head formula should be deliberate.

✔ Rely on your observation for the correct proportions of the human figure. The head as a unit of measure is convenient when you are starting to learn figure proportions.

✔ The methods illustrated are to assist designers and students of fashion to develop figure drawing when designing and presenting work. To progress is to study anatomy and attend life drawing classes. However, you may achieve good results using the following methods for design drawing.

✔ Study the charts, note the proportions of the figure then put the charts away and try sketching the figure with a free line value.

Average Proportions 7$^{1/2}$ - 8 head measurements

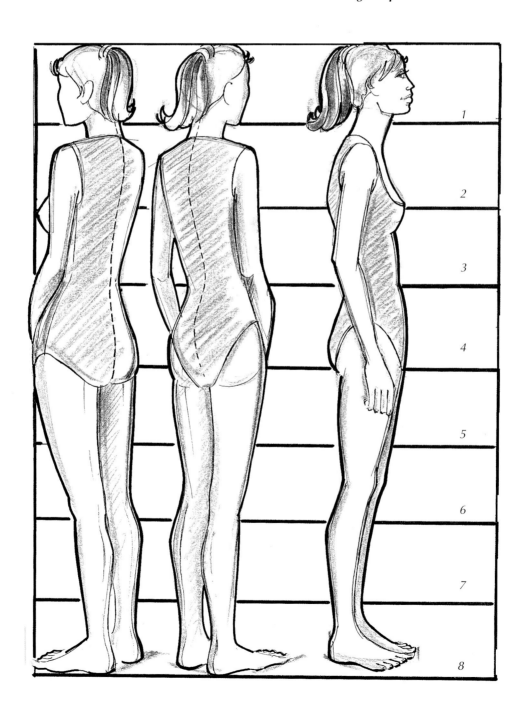

1
2
3
4
5
6
7
8

Exaggerated Features

Once you can draw a figure accurately you will have more understanding of exaggeration of fashion figures.

A designer when drawing distorts the proportions of a figure to make a statement. For example, a designer may wish to put emphasis on the shoulders by enlarging them or minimise the waist and hips or elongate the length of the figure to suggest elegance and sophistication.

Figure distortions are used to promote through the drawing a designer's fashion image, emphasising the silhouette, line, and style features.

Creating the correct image depends on how you present the drawing. Consideration would be given to the pose reflecting the occasion, i.e. sporty, elegant or sophisticated. The accessories and hairstyle are important features, they need only to be suggested to create the total look.

Exaggerated Proportions
8-8¹/₂ head measurements with the extra length added on the legs

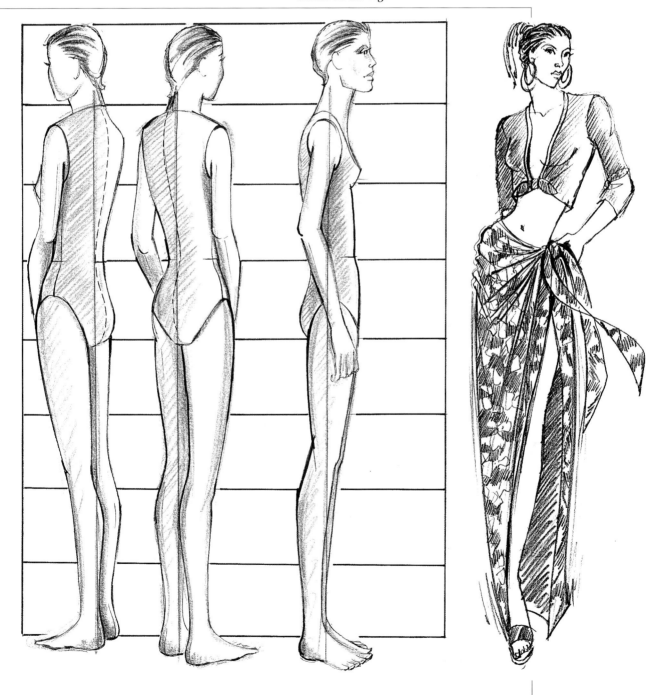

Sketch book:

Observe and sketch a varied selection of fabrics when draped and gathered.
It is an advantage to drape the fabrics on a dress stand or model. Experiment with different media using line, line and watercolour wash or coloured pencils.

Proportions 8¹/₂ head measurements

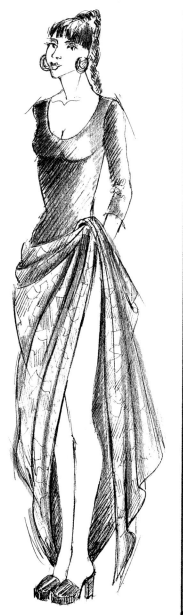

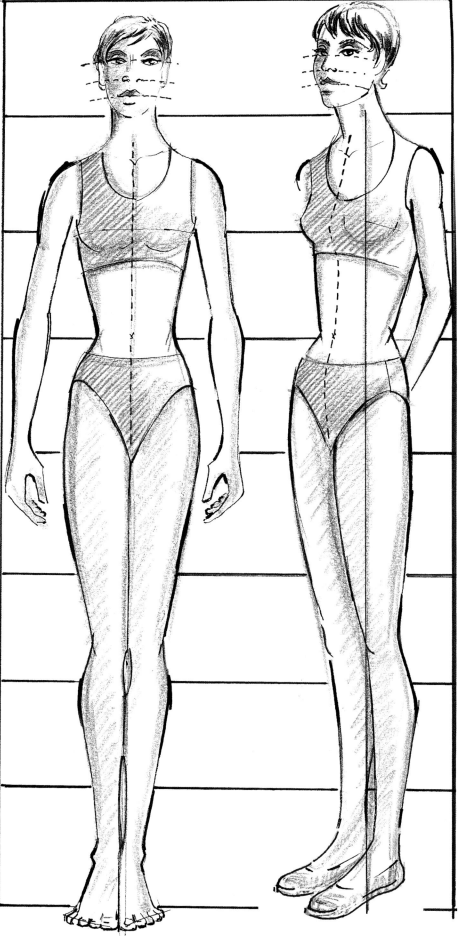

Drawing the Figure

Use the head as the basic unit of measurement for drawing the entire figure. The head may be viewed when drawing both in terms of its width and height.

The head is used from the chin to the top of the skull for vertical measurements, the width of the head for horizontal measurements. The shoulders are three widths across.

✔ To give volume to your figure drawing is to feel the shapes as you observe and draw them.

✔ When developing fashion sketches from imagination, draw round the shapes, consider the basic cylindrical, tubular and spherical parts of which the body is made up.

✔ The human body is made up of simple solid forms. It is helpful to think in terms of simple basic forms and understanding the essential masses of the separate parts and placing them in their correct proportions and relationships. Think of the form of the figure as if it were made of solid separate sections.

✔ At this stage ignore hair and features as well as the more subtle curves of the figure resulting from underlying bone and muscle structure.

✔ Once you have an understanding of the basic forms you will follow with drawing the details of the figure.

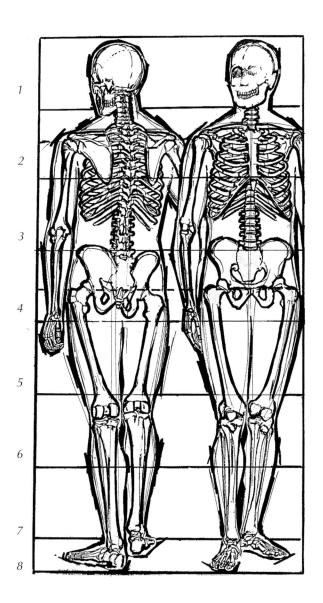

The Spine and Neck

Shoulder
Ball and Socket

Elbow
Hinge Joint

Hips Balland Socket

Wrist Ball and Socket

Knee Hinge Joint

Ankle Ball and Socket

✔ The female's shoulders are narrow and sloping with wide hips.

✔ The male is broad shouldered and relatively narrow at the hips.

✔ The fashion design drawing tends to dictate the shape of the figure depending on the cut and style of the garment and the image the designer is creating.

✔ Note the points at which motion occurs.

✔ The individual parts are connected by three very different types of joints.
Ball and Socket –
(Shoulders - Hips - Wrist - Ankles)
Hinge Joint – (Knees - Elbows)
The Flexible Column – (Spine and Neck)

Develop the figure in different poses working from the basic shapes. Sketching with a soft 3B pencil in a free style

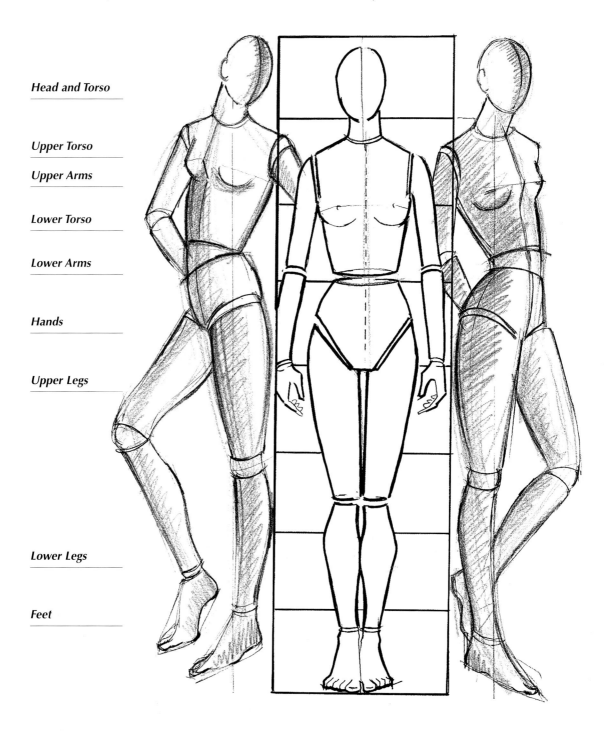

Head and Torso

Upper Torso

Upper Arms

Lower Torso

Lower Arms

Hands

Upper Legs

Lower Legs

Feet

Exaggerated Proportions

Exaggerated proportions are often used for fashion illustration to promote a particular image. When sketching a design, the pose of the figure, facial features, hairstyle and design details are emphasised to create a strong image. This highly stylised technique is often used when presenting designs not only for promotional purposes but also for exhibitions, window displays and editorial articles.

✔ Classical Greek figures were eight heads in height. The head being used as the unit of measure.

✔ The average figure is *7½* heads. In fashion drawing the proportions are often exaggerated.

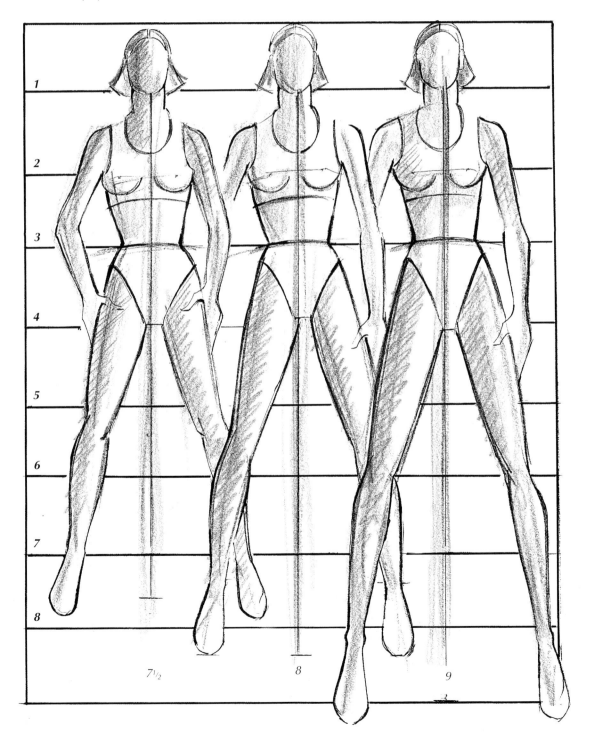

✔ The figures are elongated to project a particular image.

✔ Should you stylise or caricature a drawing and increase the height from 7 to 8 , 9 or 10 heads in height, the emphasis is usually on the length of the legs.

✔ Note the exaggeration of the length of the legs developed from the basic proportions.

✔ When exaggerating the proportions and elongating the figure to achieve a particular fashion image retain the same measurements used to draw the eight head figure but increase the length of the legs.

✔ After drawing in the head, position sketch other parts of the figure along the vertical axis line from neck to feet elongating the figure for the effect you require.

✔ The pose suggested is very important related to promotional and presentation drawings to present the correct fashion image through the drawing.

Proportions 9 head measurements

Drawing from Life

One of the most important things to observe related to proportions is that of making sure the figure is standing correctly. The distribution of the figure's weight taken by one leg or both has to be established. In order to do this check by drawing lightly a vertical line from the pit of the neck to the ankle on which most of the weight is taken.

When sketching from a model in a standing position, it is much harder for even an experienced model to keep the pose for a long period of time. Most fashion design courses have special periods allotted to life and fashion drawing. The length of the poses will vary from between five and twenty minutes. It is helpful if you can persuade a friend to model for you to give you extra time and practise in drawing from life.

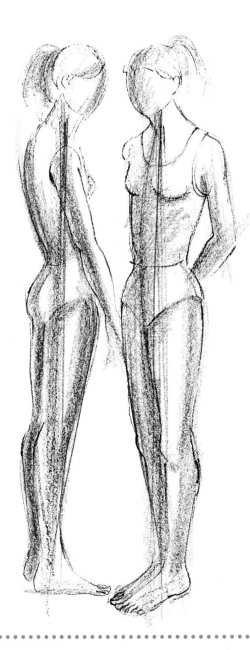

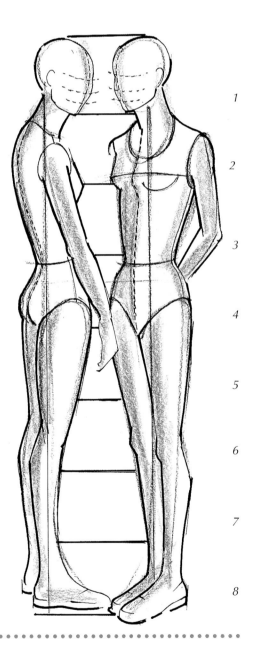

Stage 1: Teenage figures sketched in a free style working from a model (10 min sketch)

Stage 2: Drawing overlaid with layout paper and traced selecting a minimum of lines to produce a simple line drawing

Stage 3: Fashion sketches produced using template as a guide. A Softcolour black Stabilo pencil using different pressures for tone values. Sketched on a textured cartridge drawing paper.

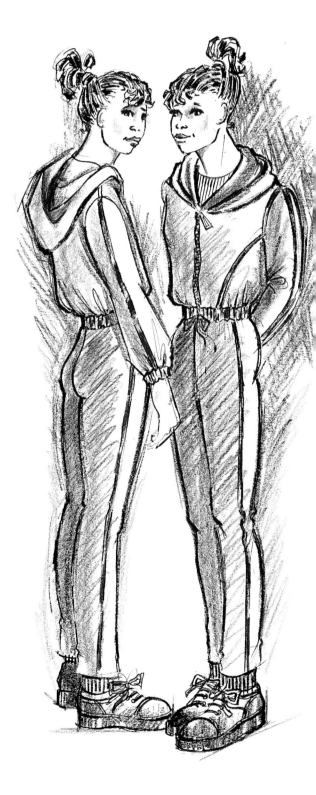

Drawing from a Model

Develop your drawing skills working from the model. If you are unable to attend classes ask a friend to model for you.

Start by sketching quick poses of five to ten minutes, observe the main points of the pose without going into great detail. Experiment developing the drawings working with different media from pencils, charcoal, pastels to watercolours and mixed media. Try working with different papers, colour, texture and weight.

Drawing on a larger scale is helpful when working with charcoal or pastels enabling you to work in a free style.

Working from a model a 30 min drawing using a charcoal pencil on pastel paper. A soft pliable rubber was used to lift areas of tone in the drawing

*Seated figure. Pen and ink sketch working on
a smooth surface Bristol board with a soft pastel
for shading*

Sketch developed from a model working in a free style with a pale grey Pantone Marker pen. Then working into the tone with a fine line Stabilo pen point 88 fine 0.4 to emphasise the details on a smooth white drawing Bristol board

Head of model sketched on a large sheet of tinted pastel paper as a mid-tone using a soft 3B lead pencil with a pale grey Pantone Marker pen for tone. This is an effective media to use when producing quick sketches

Sketch of seated figure produced on a sheet of white layout paper with a Schwan black Stabilo Softcolour pencil. A pale grey Pantone Marker pen for shading. For the details a Stabilo point 88 fine 0.4 drawing pen

Working from Photographs

Drawing the basic figure

From magazines select photographs suitable for figure reference preferably photographs which give a clear indication of the figure; swimwear being an ideal example. Use the photographs as a guide only, adapting them as required to produce a simple figure sketch.

✔ Working from a photograph or a model first study the pose, note the leg which is taking the weight of the figure and the tilt of the shoulders and hips.

✔ Start by sketching lines that indicate the size, proportions and gesture or action.

✔ Sketch using a free line or shading, many of the lines will be covered or erased as the drawing develops.

✔ When working from a photograph select one illustrating swimwear enabling you to sketch the figure.

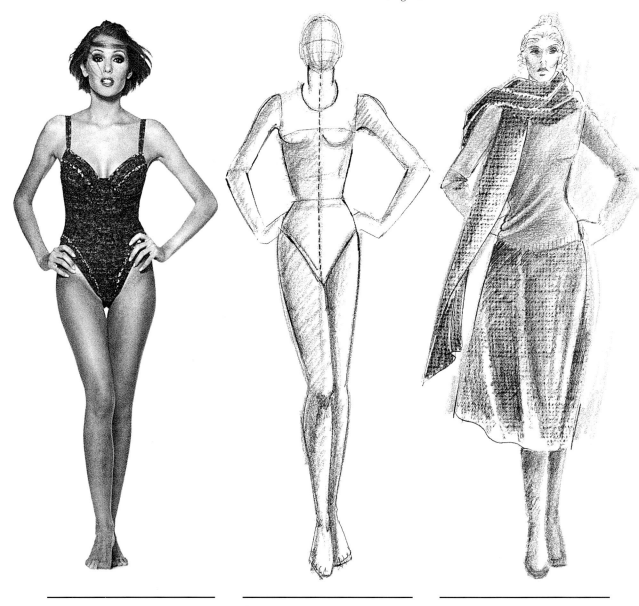

Stage 1   Stage 2   Stage 3

Design developed over the templates

Stage 1

Stage 3. Fashion sketches using smooth layout paper. The frottage technique was used for texture by placing hessian under the layout paper and applying a wax crayon over the surface of the paper. Note the areas left white to give the feeling of light

Stage 2. Quick sketches developed from a photograph of models wearing swimwear. Using a very soft 4B lead pencil in a free style drawing the impression of the pose

Designing on Computers

Designing and illustrating with the aid of computer graphics and printout facilities have provided more scope for design innovation.

Designs are instantly developed enabling the designer to experiment with line, colour, texture and proportions. A variety of graphic techniques may be achieved from a variation of line values, brush strokes, marker pens, pastel and watercolour.

The effects also include a selection of paper textures, airbrush and a vast selection of colour variations instantly produced.

Stage 1: Scan Figure template and bring it on screen

Stage 2: Sketch design over image of figure template

Stage 3: Hide figure template

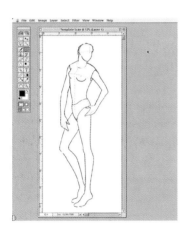

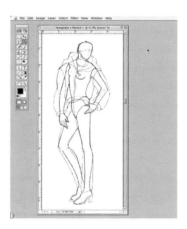

Computer graphics are included in most fashion design and marketing courses enabling the student to develop the skills required improving creativity at the touch of a keyboard.

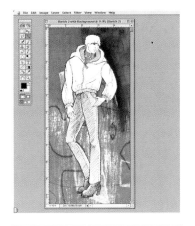

Stage 4: Completed sketch

Stage 5: Completed sketch with background effect

Drawing from Imagination

When developing the figure from imagination it is important to view the body in terms of simple basic, solid volumes which can move in relation to one another before developing details and subtlety of form. The form should be seen as simple blocks based on the cube, cylinder or sphere. This conception of the figure as a series of simple masses is most valuable in constructing imaginative figures seen from different angles.

Templates may be developed by tracing over the constructed figure drawing and simplifying the lines as illustrated. With practise an individual style will be developed, often referred to as a designer's handwriting.

✔ 1. When developing the figure from imagination it is important to view the body in terms of simple basic forms and understanding the proportions.

✔ 2. Sketch the figure from imagination keeping the solidity of the forms in mind. The pose is exaggerated on the length of the legs and developed as a template.

✔ 3. Select pose most suitable for the design. Place the simple line figure template under the semi-transparent layout paper or use a light box.

Sketch book: As an exercise, sketch a selection of shoes with a variation of heels. When worn, note how the height of the heel changes the shape and position of the foot.

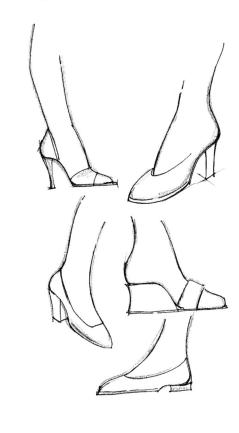

Stage 1

Pencil sketches developed freely over the figures. Shading with Schwan Stabilo Softcolour Pencils using different pressure for tonal values on a *textured cartridge paper. Note the areas of white to give the effect of light on the figures. The fine details added with a Stabilo pen point 88 fine 0.4*

Stage 2

Stage 3

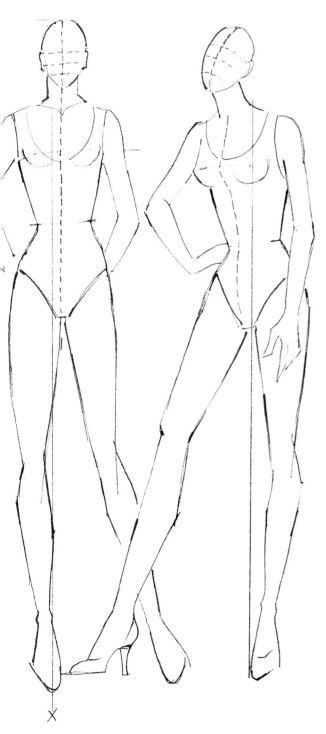

✔ Articulated lay figures are available in several sizes used as an aid for developing figure poses. They are wooden forms based on the cylinder, cube and sphere. The most important blocks are the rib cage and pelvic area which govern the position and direction of the blocks representing the neck, head and limbs. The joints are articulated enabling different figure positions to be created.

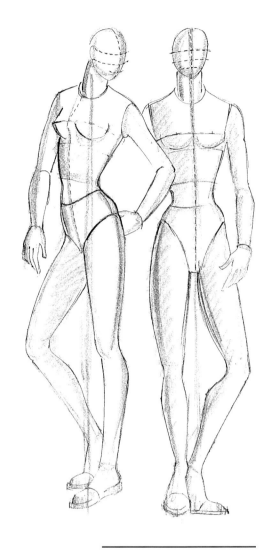

Stage 2: Development of figures as templates

Stage 1: Figures sketched with a soft 4B pencil developing figures based on the cylinder, cub and sphere

Stage 3:
Design sketch over template

Stage 4: Fashion sketches developed over the figure template using a layout paper with a black Softcolour Stabilo pencil for shading. The tweed effects achieved by placing a textured canvas under the paper and rubbing the pencil over the surface of the paper using different pressure for tone values. Darker tones to emphasise the collar and folds

How to use the Template

The figure template is a tool for working when designing. The advantage of the template in the early stages of design drawing is to enable design ideas to be expressed quickly on to the paper.

The figure need only be an indication of the pose and proportions of the figure on which to develop designs. This should not influence the drawing and techniques used.

When designing and developing ideas for a collection, many quick sketches are produced before making a final selection.

✔ Sketch over the figure image through the paper using a free line technique with a B or 2B lead pencil developing the design sketch. The figure should not be traced, use only as a guide for the pose and the proportions. Once the impression of the sketch is established remove the template and complete the drawing.

✔ Suggest the face and hairstyle suitable for the fashion image, keep the details simple in the early stages of working.

✔ The hands and footwear need only be suggested. Make sure the hand is the correct size, check the hand related to the size of the face.

✔ Make sure the figure is standing correctly (check the axis line from the pit of the neck to the floor indicating the leg taking the weight of the figure).

✔ Use the centre front line indicating the contour of the body. This line helps considerably when balancing design details, i.e. pockets, seams, placing of zips and buttons, etc.

A very simple basic figure template was used

Design sketch illustrating the complete image with back view and sample fabrics. Notes may also be added if required. A collection of design sketches would be presented in the same size and format making it easy to view when presenting work to a client or for interviews

The drawing has been produced with a black Stabilo Softcolour pencil, a Pantone Marker pen by Letraset was used for the jacket. The trousers textured with a wax crayon. Details of seams, pockets, etc. added with a very fine 0.5 Pilot Ball Point pen. Note the areas of white left to emphasise the details of the jacket

Developing Design Ideas

Many sketches are produced in the early stages before selecting a collection of designs. This process is often referred to as "Brain Storming". The designer works on a theme researching ideas and selecting colours and fabrics to create the overall image.

✔ A simple front and back figure template with a straight on view of the pose enables the designer to work quickly and accurately developing designs relating one design to another when working on a theme.

✔ Use the same pose repeated a number of times including the back view of the design.

✔ It is not always required to sketch the full figure when designing swimwear, jackets and tops.

✔ A simple indication of the face, hands or shoes are only required when developing design ideas. A more detailed and illustrative drawing would be produced when presenting design collections, promotional work and for competitions.

Development of design ideas working with the same figure pose enabling you to work quickly when designing and working on a theme

Black wax crayon - Pantone Marker pen - Fine pointed black pencil for the details

Women – Templates

✔ Develop one figure pose into a variation of poses by changing the position of the relaxed leg leaving the other leg to take the weight of the body.

✔ Sketch over the original pose or develop the poses free hand.

Sketch book: Experiment sketching figures freehand developing different poses. Emphasise the length of the legs, the angles of the shoulders and hips. Remember to check the balance line from the neck to the foot, taking the weight of the body. When tracing over the templates slim the figures down adapting the pose for the effect you require.

Experiment with pencils and textures of paper. It is effective to use a combination of soft 3B-4B lead pencils for shading to a sharper line value for the finer details B-HB

✔ Select the pose to reflect the mood or activity of the design.

✔ Consider the angles of the pose to illustrate certain design features.

✔ Check the figure is standing correctly, note which leg is taking the weight of the figure.

✔ Use the centre front line as a guide to balance the design features.

Quick sketches produced with a fine pointed black Pentel Drawing pen on a smooth surface paper

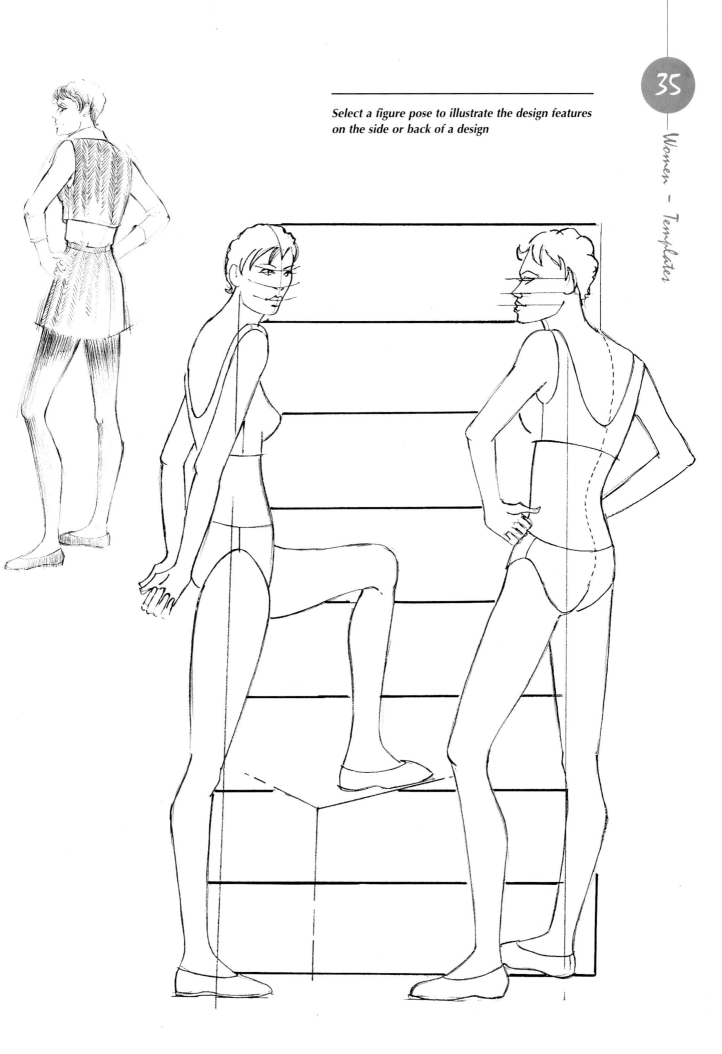

Select a figure pose to illustrate the design features on the side or back of a design

✔ Stylised figures with extra length on the legs
giving a more exaggerated image. Experiment
with the proportions of the figure to achieve
the fashion statement you wish to project
through the sketch.

*Develop sketches freehand experimenting with a
selection of poses. Always check which leg is taking
the weight of the figure for the correct balance*

Note how the few simple lines sketched over the figure indicate the dress following the curves of the figure

Line and Wash

As a progression it is interesting to experiment with different media. Use different drawing and painting techniques to indicate colour, pattern and texture. A varied selection of Art materials is available including watercolours, designer gouache, coloured pencils, marker pens, inks and pastels.

When working with different media be sure to select suitable paper on which to apply the colour otherwise the experimenting may result in disappointment. For the best results always use good quality brushes, mix the colours in a clean pallet and use plenty of clean water.

✔ The line and wash technique is particularly suited for quick fashion design sketches.

✔ One method is to begin with a pen or pencil drawing then apply with a brush a watercolour wash leaving areas of the sketch white. When using this technique you should avoid filling in the sketch to look like a colouring book exercise. It is often more effective to apply the washes in a free manner, then work into the sketch with more detail with a pen or pencil if necessary.

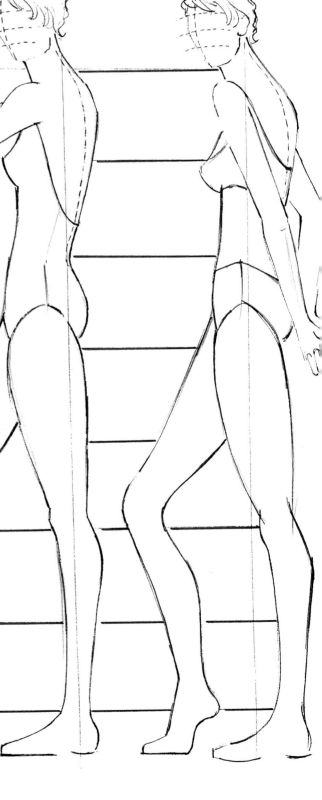

Design sketches produced over templates using a very fine waterproof drawing pen adding a watercolour wash to suggest the folds and drapery

Light and Tone

It is effective when developing a sketch to indicate the main direction of light on the figure by adding areas of tone that are not directly lit.

This may be achieved with pencil shading, marker pens or a watercolour wash. The effects can be dramatic and will give the drawing volume.

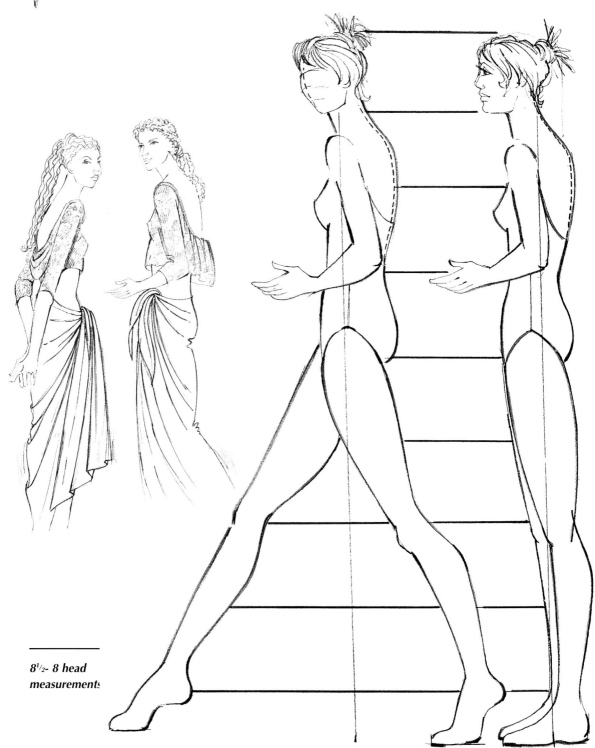

8¹/₂- 8 head measurements

Effects of folds and drapery may be easily achieved by adding light and tone to the sketch. A Pantone Marker pen has been applied to give contrast and depth to the folds.

Templates – Presentation

The presentation of design work is very important and should be carefully considered. When presenting work for an assessment or competition, or when preparing a portfolio for an interview, a student should give careful thought to the organisation of the material making it easy to view.

✔ Casual poses illustrating sports leisure wear garments.

✔ Sketches produced using the templates.

✔ 8½ head measurement into the figure.

✔ Pencils and black Schwan Stabilo Softcolour pencils. For finer details, seams, pockets, buttons and belt Pilot Hi Tecpoint V7 fine pen.

✔ A free pencil shading on trousers and boots in contrast to the more controlled technique in other areas of the sketch.

Sketch book: When planning the layout of the design work for presentation, sketch a selection of rough layout ideas before making a final arrangement. Consider the most suitable figure poses to present the designs.

Presentation Board

✔ The same pose has been adapted and reversed. Figures cut out and mounted onto card against a photograph to suggest the mood.

✔ The working drawings produced with a fine pointed Pilot Hi Tecpoint V5.

✔ Experiment with layout and presentation effects before making the final decisions (by hand or on the computer).

Frottage

✔ This technique is used in drawing to obtain textured effects and shading by placing a texture under a sheet of paper and rubbing or drawing across the surface of the paper with a soft pencil or crayon.

✔ This effect can be produced from almost any firm textured surface on which you can place your paper.

✔ A thin layout paper or thin cartridge is suitable to achieve the textural effect through the paper.

Textures produced using hessian, leather, nets, wire mesh and canvas. It is effective when using this technique to leave areas of white and add darker tones as illustrated

Note how the same pose has been used to illustrate a selection of designs

✔ Regard the head as a egg shape.
When suggesting the face and head in a
fashion sketch it is essential to work from the
basic proportions first. Divide the main

features into thirds (as illustrated). The features
need only be suggested when design
sketching, a more detailed effect may be
developed for presentation work.

Sketch book: Sketch faces from a model
or photographs working from different angles.
Keep the sketches simple.

Frottage

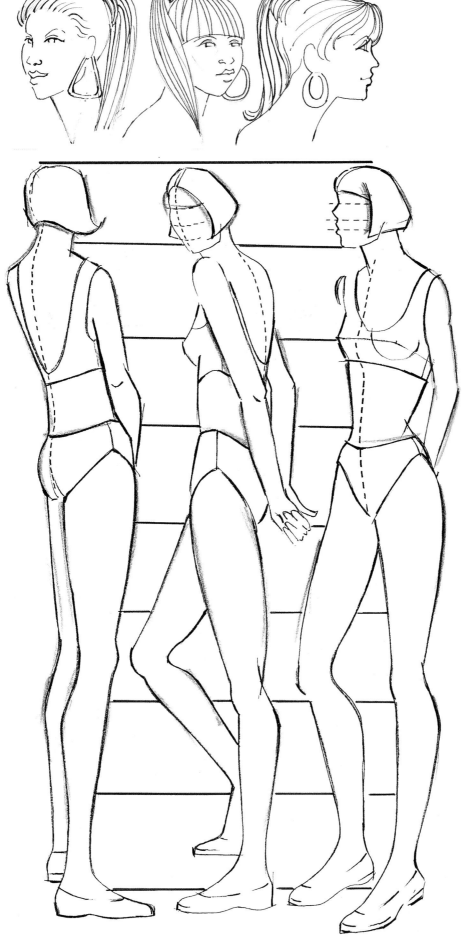

Sketch book:
Practise drawing the
hairstyles and faces as
seen from different
angles. Keep the
sketches to a simple
line value.

✔ Two stages developing a sketch.

✔ Figure exaggerated on the length of the legs.

✔ Softcolour Stabilo pencils used for shading on a textured surface drawing paper.

✔ Different pressures applied with the pencils to give contrast tone values.

✔ Areas of white left on the figure suggesting contrasting light.

Sketch suggesting tweed textures and ribbing with a Stabilo point 88 fine 0.4 pen. Figure poses used from facing page

Frottage

Keep a reference in your sketchbook of new styles of footwear

✔ Note the three different hairstyles indicated with a few selected lines. Study current hairstyles, make notes and sketches in your sketch book for future reference.

✔ Note the development of one pose by changing the left leg position.

Sketch produced using two drawing pens providing different line values and wax crayons for the shading

Frottage

Techniques - Very exaggerated poses with extra leg length. Sketches produced with a fine pointed Stabilo pencil on a thin layout paper

✔ Experiment sketching one design onto different poses.

✔ Select figure poses suitable for the design, concentrate on sketching the design from different angles.

✔ Observe the effects of one design as seen on a variety of figures and poses.

✔ Note how the angles of the skirt and top change direction. This can be effective when slightly exaggerated in the sketch.

Textures achieved using frottage techniques placing nets under the paper and applying a soft pencil over the surface of the paper producing a transparent effect to the skirts

Presentation Board – Collage

Collage is an effective way of introducing pattern, texture and areas of flat colour. The techniques vary, from using neat paper cutout shapes to abstract and torn pieces, collage may also be combined with different media using, for instance, fabrics and photographs. This technique is used successfully for promotional presentations, textiles and fashion forecasting.

✔ Fabrics photocopied and reduced to scale. Then the shapes are cut out and applied to the sketch using Spray Mount adhesive, leaving areas of white. If the sketch is filled in the effect tends to look rather solid. Experiment with the shapes until you achieve the effects you require.

✔ Note the background is a small section of a photograph enlarged on the photocopier.

Folds and drapery effects achieved with collage techniques

Collage is the use of cut and torn paper of neat or abstract shapes applied to the drawing

✔ When design sketching it is important to express and develop your design ideas and convey the feel of the fabrics, expressing the characteristics of the fabric with a few lines.

✔ Study the way the fabric reacts according to the movement of the body. As a model moves the folds of the fabric will change in shape.

✔ The tube of a sleeve remains uncreased while the arm is straight but as soon as the elbow is bent the fabric folds and is stretched. The same occurs to any other close fitting part of a garment, so consider the type and weight of fabric you are suggesting. They vary from clinging, while others drape, gather and fall into deep folds or are reluctant to drape.

9 head measurements

Sketch book: Make some study sketches representing fabrics for reference.

Adapting a Pose

From one figure pose a number of variations may be developed by overlaying the figure with layout paper and sketching over the impression of the figure creating different stance by changing the position of the legs, arms or angle of the head.

✔ Develop from one pose a number of variations by changing the position of the arms, legs or angle of the head.

✔ Suggest different hairstyles. Check the foot or feet taking the weight of the figure. The foot shape and position will change depending on the style of footwear you suggest.

✔ Use the centre front dotted line as a guide indicating the contour line of the body to balance fashion details.

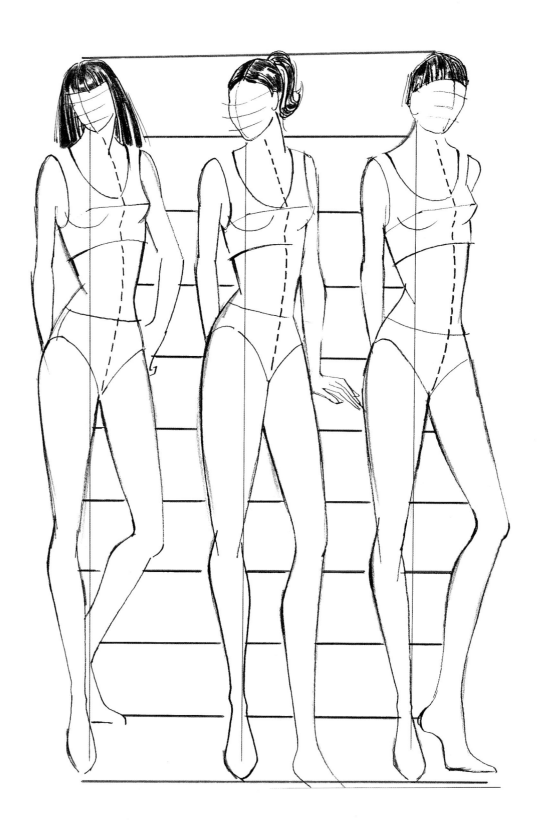

Men – Templates

Drawing the Figure

The height of the average male figure varies from between 7 to 8 heads.

For the fashion sketch the figure is usually eight to eight and a half with the length of the legs exaggerated. Try not to exaggerate when producing design sketches as this may distort the proportions of your design.

When developing figure templates simplify the drawing to create a clear outline.

The figure may also be scanned into a computer which enables you to develop design ideas and colour effects very quickly before making final decisions.

Average male figure proportions 7 - 8 heads

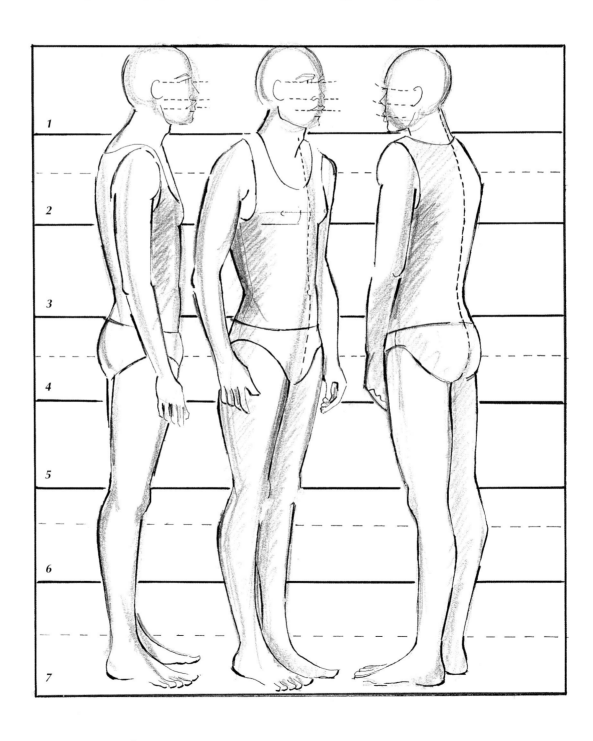

Drawing Hands

✔ Simplify the drawing of hands in a fashion sketch. The hand is often only suggested or may be concealed in a pocket or fold.

Anatomy of the hand

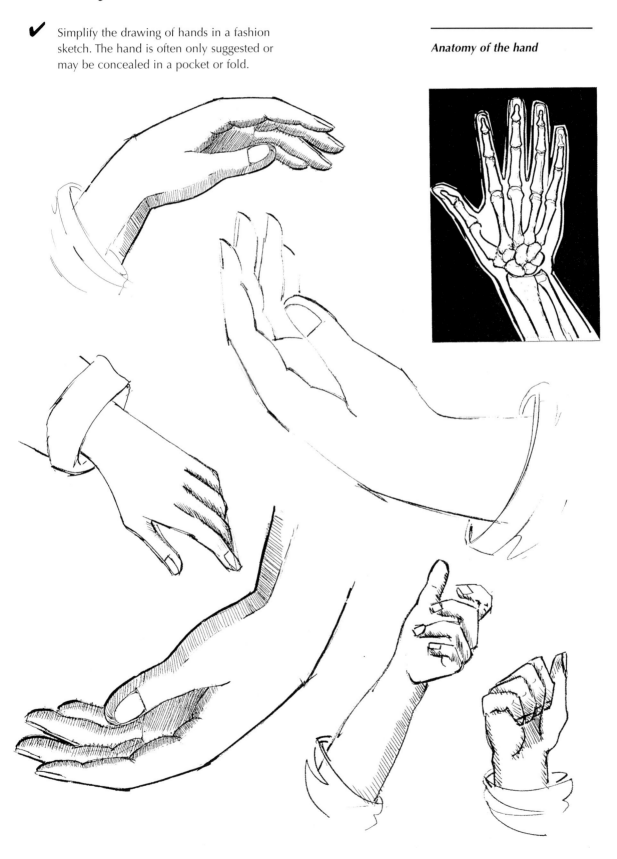

Fashion Sketches

✔ Sketches developed over the figure template. Consider the pose, face, hairstyle and footwear. These need only be suggested with a few lines when presenting a design to project the correct fashion image.

✔ Check the placement of the fashion details. The shape of a pocket, the spacing of the buttons, and cut of the collar, etc. Indicate the folds of a garment where the figure bends at the arm or knee.

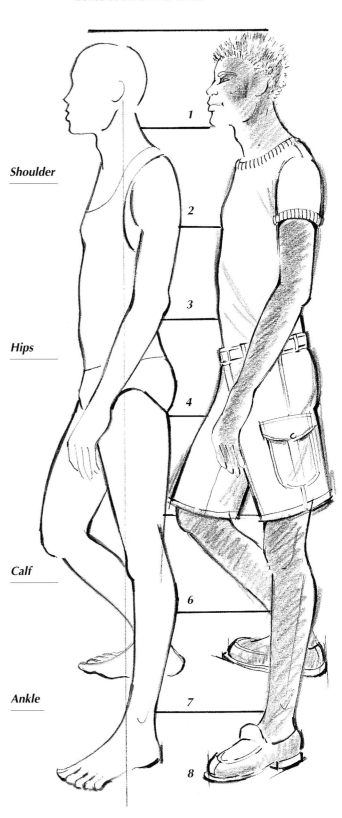

Shoulder

1

2

Hips

3

4

Calf

6

Ankle

7

8

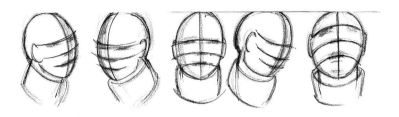

Drawing the head as seen from different angles

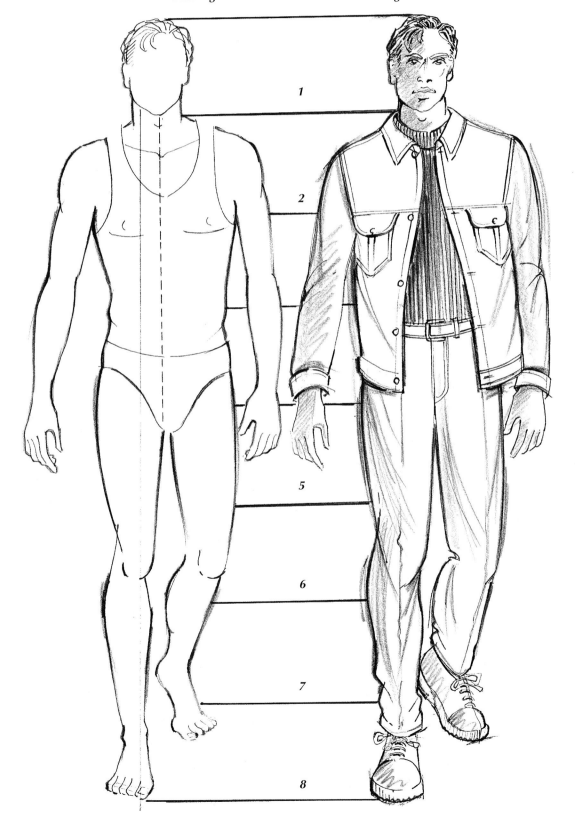

1

2

5

6

7

8

Drawing Hairstyles

✔ Hairstyles tend to date quickly, observe new trends and collect references from the latest fashion magazines.

✔ Use the figure template as a guide only. Sketch freely over the impression of the figure.

✔ Create the image you require by suggesting the correct pose, face, hairstyle and accessories.

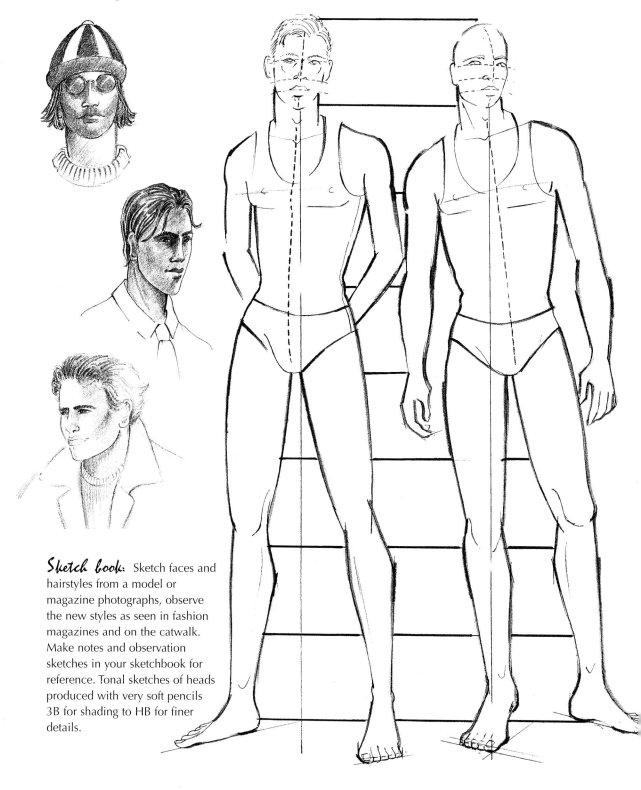

Sketch book: Sketch faces and hairstyles from a model or magazine photographs, observe the new styles as seen in fashion magazines and on the catwalk. Make notes and observation sketches in your sketchbook for reference. Tonal sketches of heads produced with very soft pencils 3B for shading to HB for finer details.

✔ It is important when presenting your design work to reflect the mood of the design by sketching the correct pose: for instance one that reflects a sports activity.

Casual wear illustrated on figures using the 8 head measurements

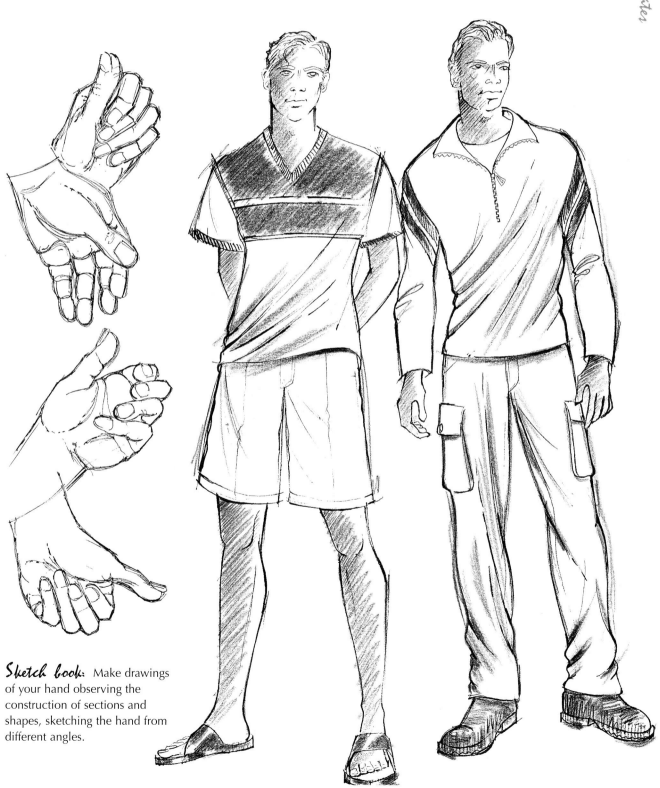

Sketch book: Make drawings of your hand observing the construction of sections and shapes, sketching the hand from different angles.

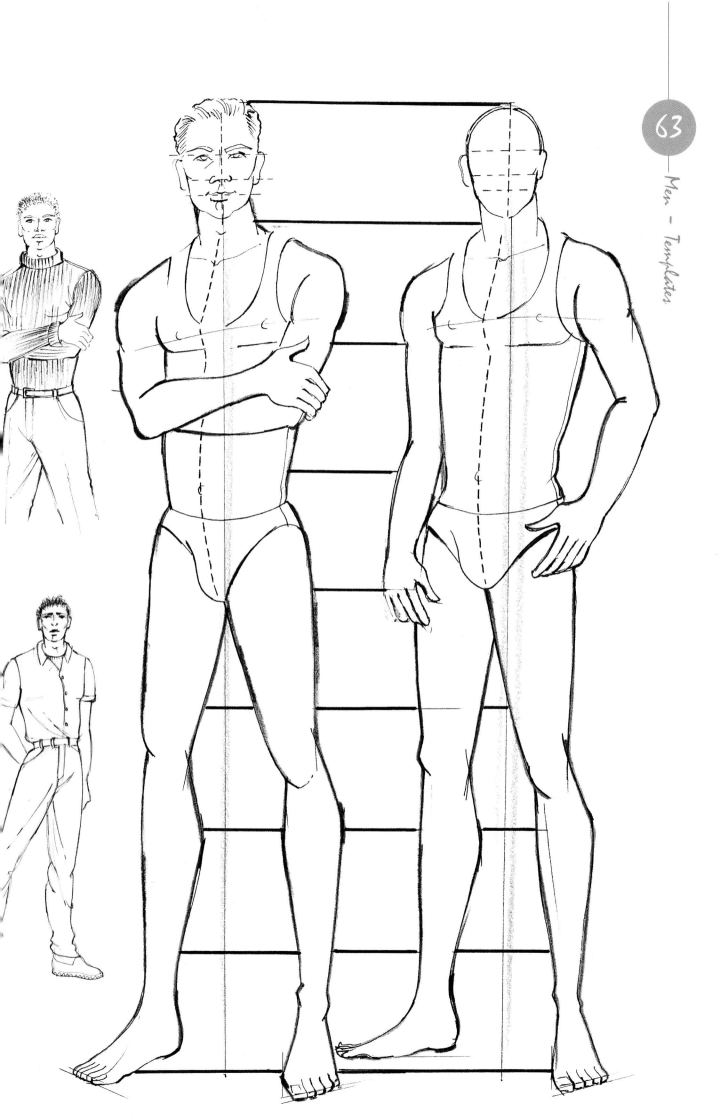

Action Poses

✔ To start, try working from templates
illustrated in the book or create some
templates of your own.

✔ Different methods can be used to achieve the
required effects: working from a model
making quick sketches which may be
developed afterwards, or working from
photographs of figures in action poses. It is
useful to take photographs for reference or
collect action photographs from sports
magazines.

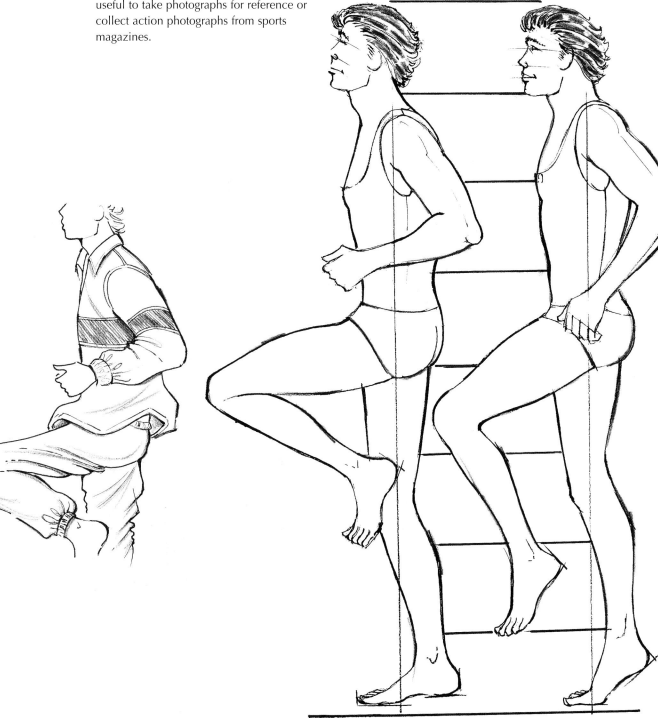

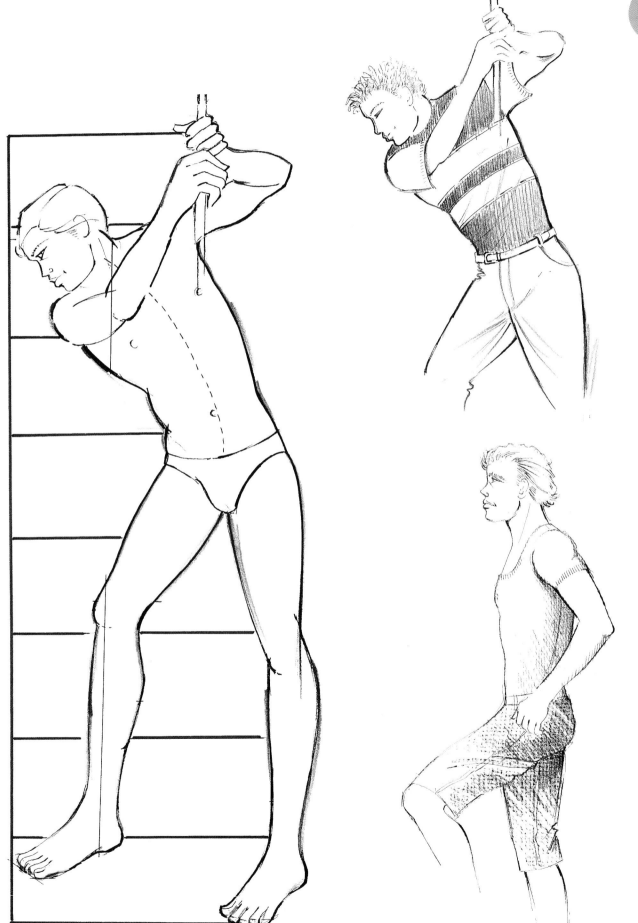

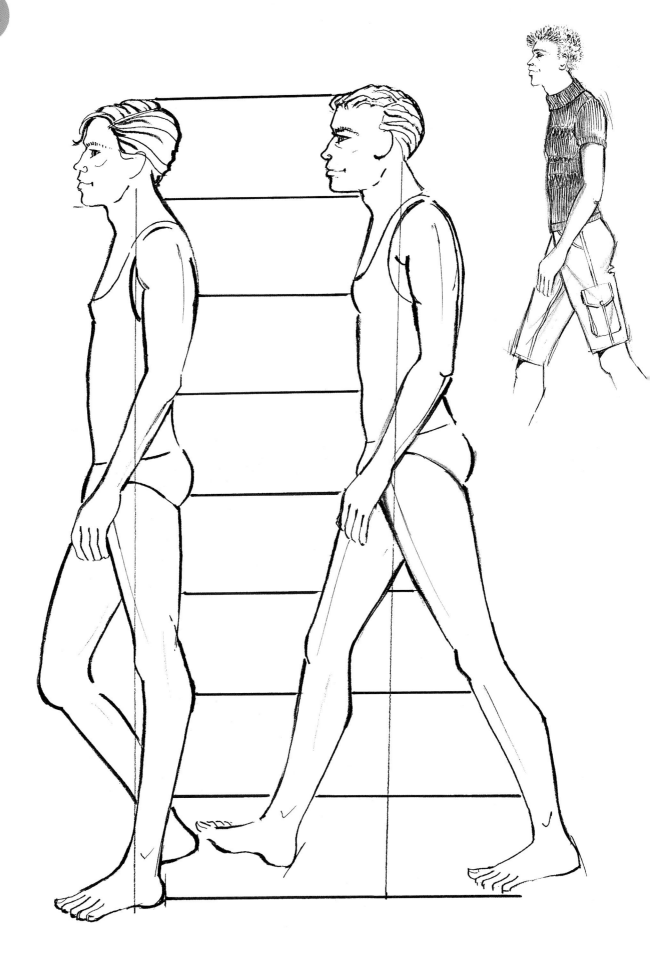

Footwear – Observation Drawing

✔ It is good practise as a student to make detailed observation drawings, this will help you considerably when using only a few lines to indicate a style of shoe or boot.

✔ Observe the new trends in shoe design. Keep a reference of current styles, note the colours, leathers and design features.

Observation drawings of shoes on a textured piece of paper produced with lead pencils 3B for shading and a B and HB for finer detail

Presentation Boards

✔ When creating presentation design sheets and boards for competitions, assessments, exhibitions or interviews, experiment with layout ideas before making final decisions. Keep constantly in touch with new graphic art materials, observe the latest magazines marketing promotions and displays.

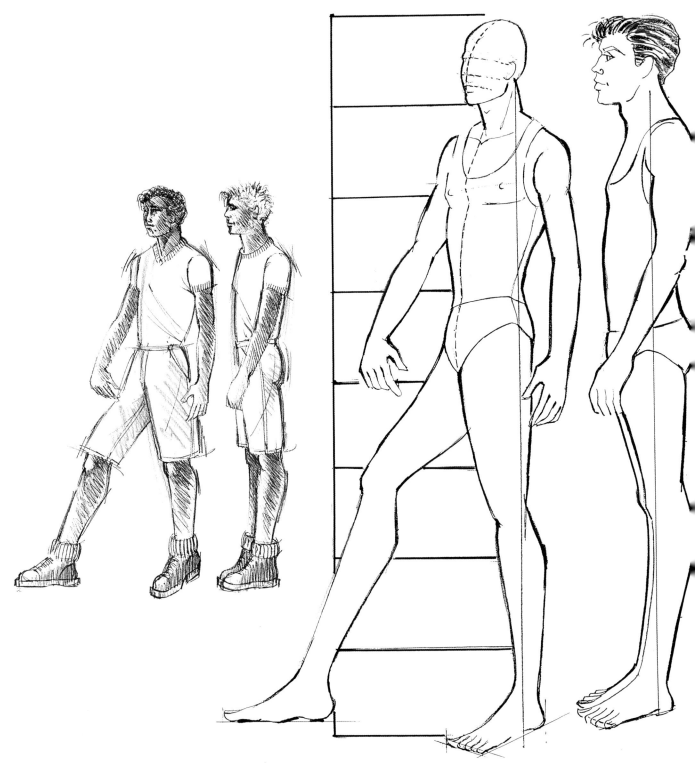

✔ The presentation of your work is important when communicating your ideas to others. Your design work should be clearly understood and presented in a professional manner.

✔ A Pantone Marker pen for tonal effects.

✔ Figures cut out and mounted on the board against a sheet of paper suggesting an airbrush effect.

✔ A section of a photograph enlarged on the photocopier used for background suggesting the mood and occasion.

Presentation board illustrating sportswear. A thick Pentel Sign pen producing a strong line combined with a fine Pilot Hi Tecpoint pen for the finer details giving contrast to the line values. Pantone Marker pens for shading, applied with a freestyle technique.

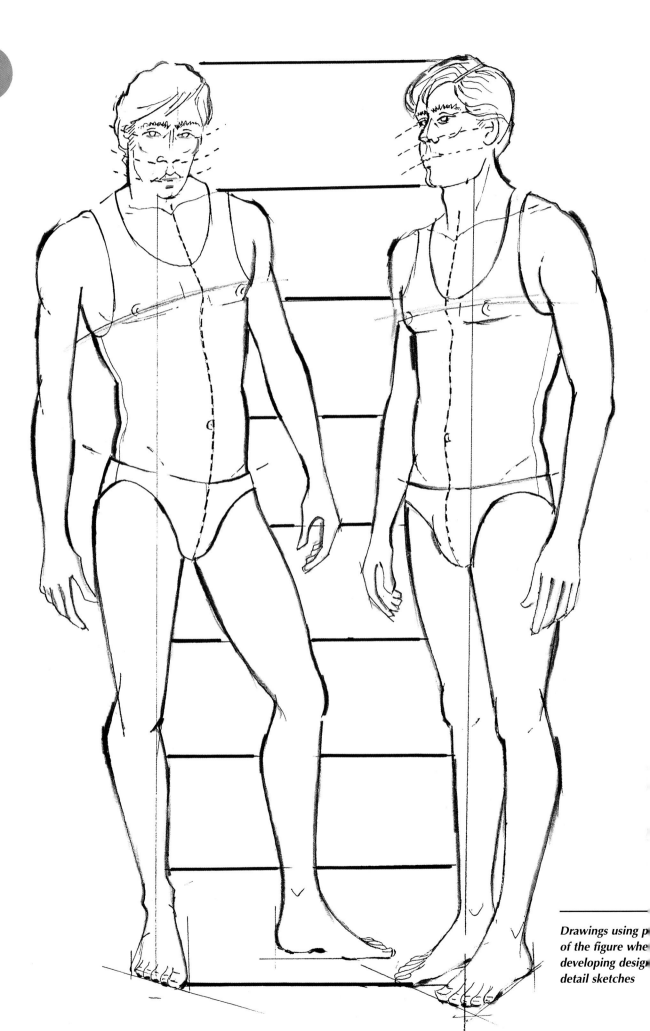

Drawings using p
of the figure whe
developing desig
detail sketches

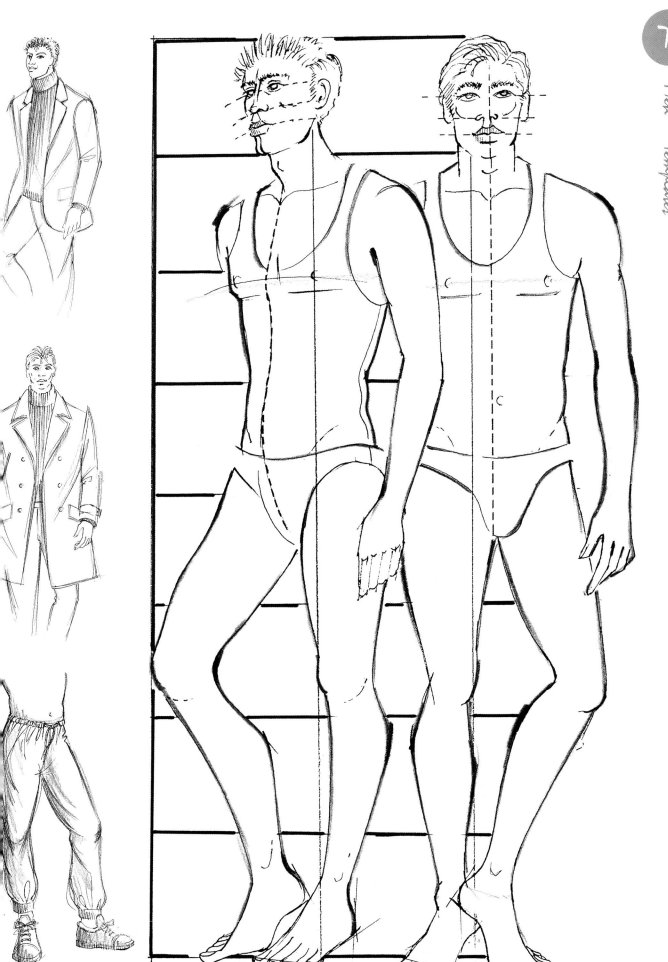

Presentation Design Board

Stage 1: Figure pose sketch from a model

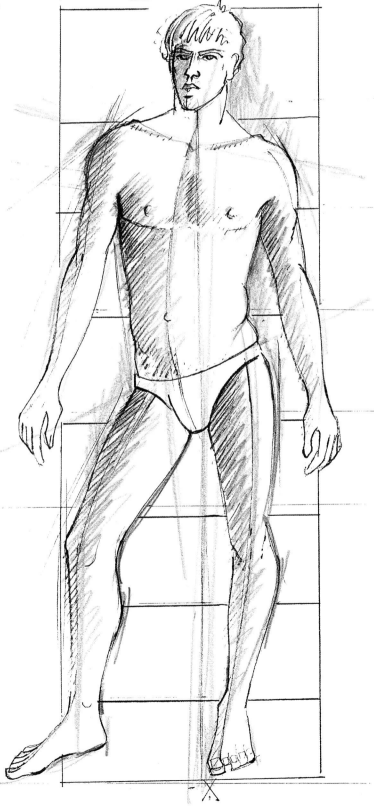

Stage 2: ine drawing of design sketch. Pose adapted by concealing the arm to the side of figure

Stage 3: Completed drawing with added texture

Stage 4: Figure cut out and spray mounted against a photographic image. The photograph was enlarged on the colour photocopier and cut out and placed in the background.

Diagramatic working drawings (flats) reduced on the photocopier or computer and mounted on the board with sample fabric.

✔ Selection of figure poses with one leg taking the weight of the body.

✔ Sketch over the impression of the figure through the paper you are using, adapting the pose to your own requirements, the figure should not be traced, use it as a guide only designing and developing ideas freely.

✔ Sketch developed from the template pose. Produced with a soft 3B pencil on layout paper.

When sketching consider the fabric you are representing and the way in which it would behave, it is helpful to think of the garment when *designing and drawing as an essential part of the figure suggesting with a few lines the movement and characteristics of the material*

Presentation Board – Sportswear

Careful detailed line drawing produced with pens of different thickness

1 *Pilot V Sign Pen for the thick line value*
2 *0.7 Pilot Ball Pen for finer line value*
3 *Pantone Marker Pen for tone applied with a free style technique*

The fashion sketch, flats, and photograph cut out and arranged against a sheet of paper suggesting an airbrush effect mounted onto a card for presentation

Airbrush DECAdry Print paper could be used for photocopiers and laser printers

Children — Templates

Proportions

It is important to be aware of the changing proportions of the growing child when drawing and designing for different age groups. There are no rules to the growth in the child. Children vary, these measurements on the charts indicate the normal average growth.

The beginner will find it helpful to work from the charts illustrated constructing the figure by calculating the number of heads that would fit into the length of the body. You also have to remember that the size of the head and the length of arms, hands, legs and feet will alter according to age.

Design sketches and illustrations for children and teenage fashion are often produced using a stylised drawing technique, some are extreme like cartoons. This can be very effective when sketching the younger age groups.

✔ During the early stages of a child's growth the infant's limbs are proportionally short, with the upper limbs at first longer than the lower.

Age 6

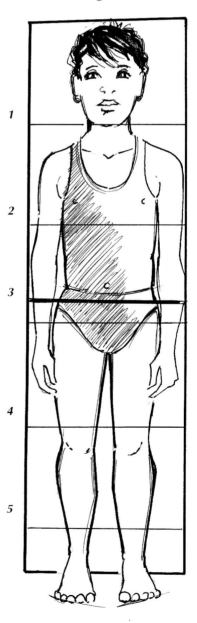

Age 3

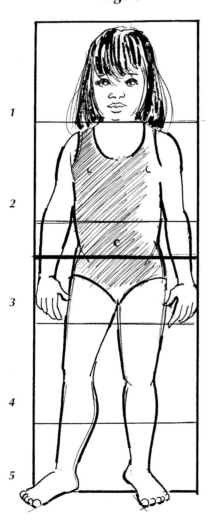

✔ A new born baby is nearly four heads high and the head is a little over a quarter of the height of its body.

✔ The figure chart illustrates the proportions of the figure measuring the head into the body.

The thick line indicates the halfway point of each individual's height which illustrates that nearly half of the adult height is in the legs.

Age 12

Age 9

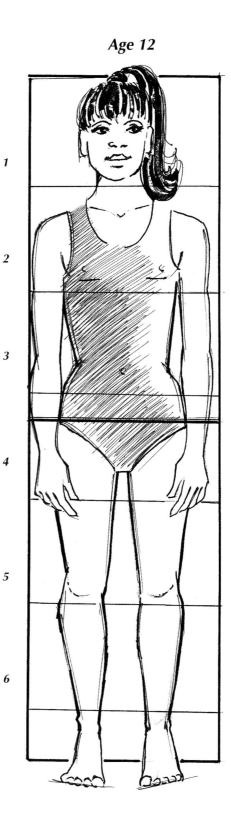

Ages One-Two

Practise sketching from life, keep a sketch book observing children and teenage attitudes. It is difficult to sketch children in a set pose as they are not patient as models. Make quick sketches from life and develop them later. Make use of a camera and develop new poses from the photographs taken.

✔ During the early stages of growth the infant's limbs are proportionally short with the upper limbs at first longer than the lower.

✔ The middle line of the body is above the navel, after two years it is on the navel, after this it is above this point.

Sketch book: Make quick sketches for reference. Observe the basic shapes and structure of the poses working with a 6B pencil.

Ages 1, 2 & 3

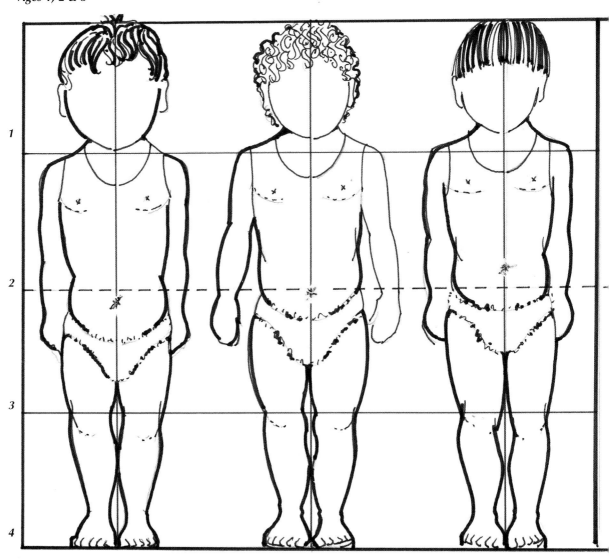

**Black drawing pen Stabilo point 88 fine 0.4
and Pantone Marker pen for tone on a smooth
Bristol board**

Age Three

Stylised sketches of children are particularly effective when designing for the younger age groups.

A few lines can suggest a pose reflecting the attitude of a child.

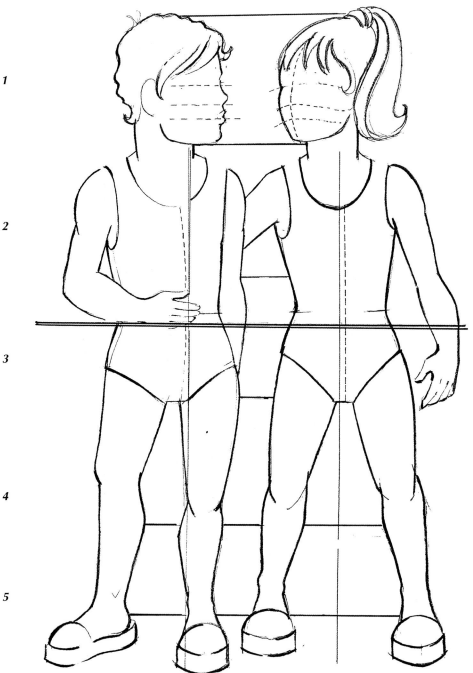

1

2

3

4

5

Sketch book: Experiment with different illustrative techniques when design drawing, from a realistic approach to highly stylised effects. Always keeping the age and proportions in mind when exaggerating the proportions of the figure for effect. Practise sketching children's shoes and boots from different angles, note the style features and the different shapes. Keep the sketches simple, this exercise will help considerably when producing design sketches working from imagination indicating the shoes with a few lines.

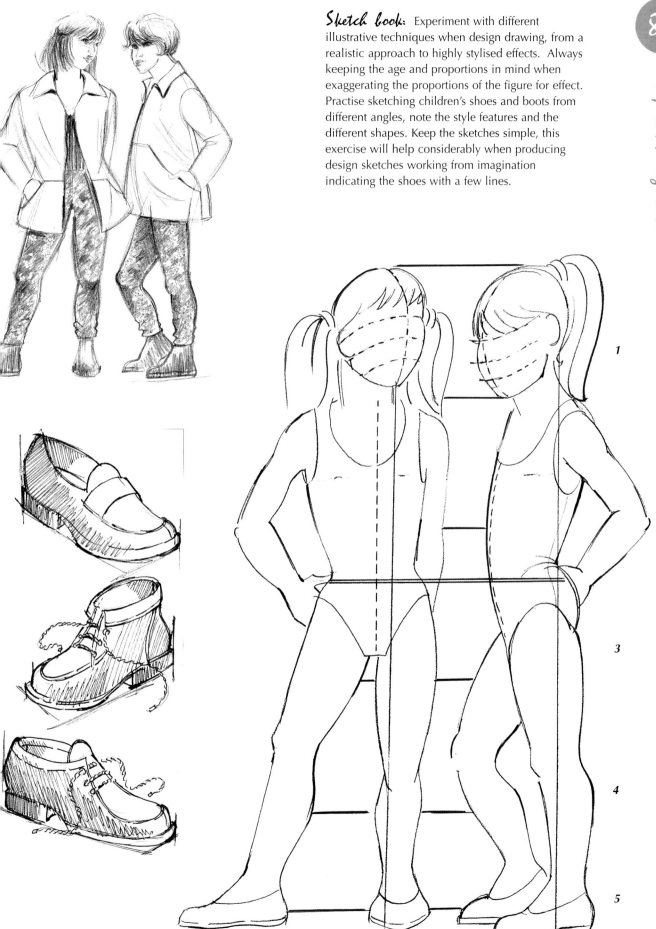

1

3

4

5

Age Five

Three figures from opposite page. Line drawing using a fine drawing pen Stabilo point 88 water solvent combined with a watercolour wash.

✔ Experiment with sketching new hairstyles using a few simple lines. Note when sketching round the egg shape of the head the hair will give more width and height to the head shape.

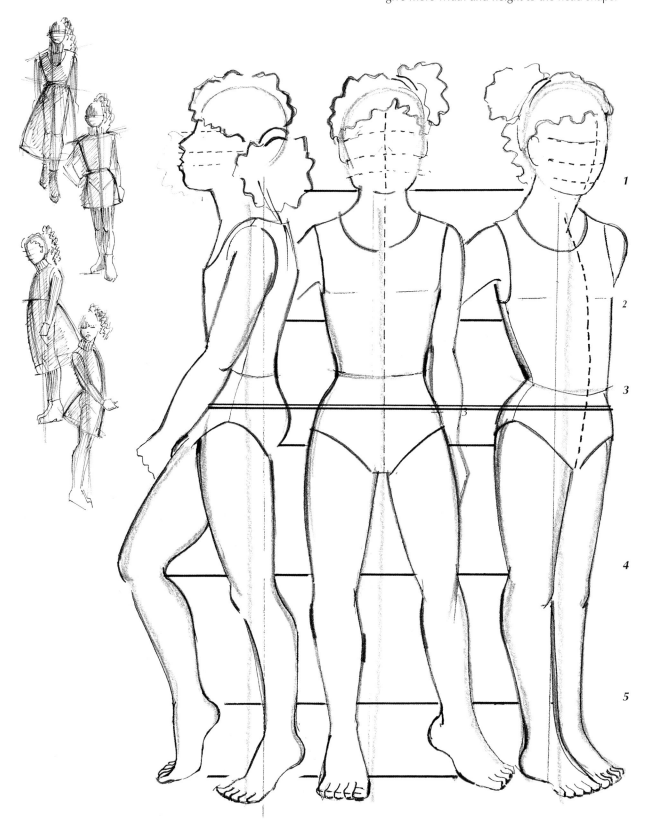

Sketch book: Practise sketching freely, developing new poses seen from different angles and attitudes. Keep the sketches simple, leaving out details. These sketches may be used for reference when producing figure poses for designing and presentation work.

Age Nine

Experiment sketching the same hairstyles seen from different poses

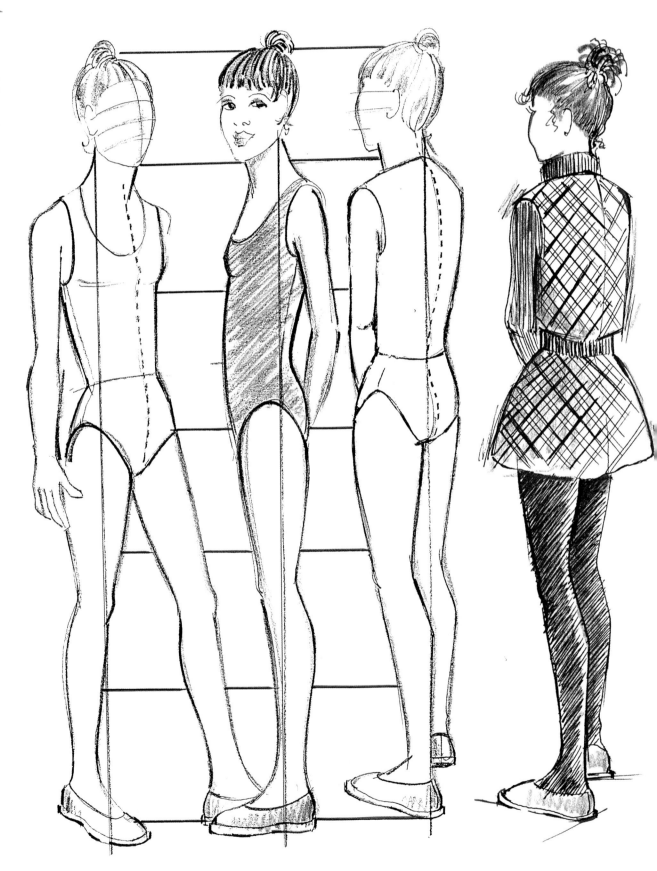

*Vary the pose, changing the position of arms, legs,
and position of the head*

1

2

3

4

5

6

Age Fifteen

✔ A soft lead pencil drawing 3B on a cartridge paper with a watercolour wash added to give the effects of tone, light, pattern and colour.

✔ A Stabilo pen point 88 fine 0.4 pen was used for details.

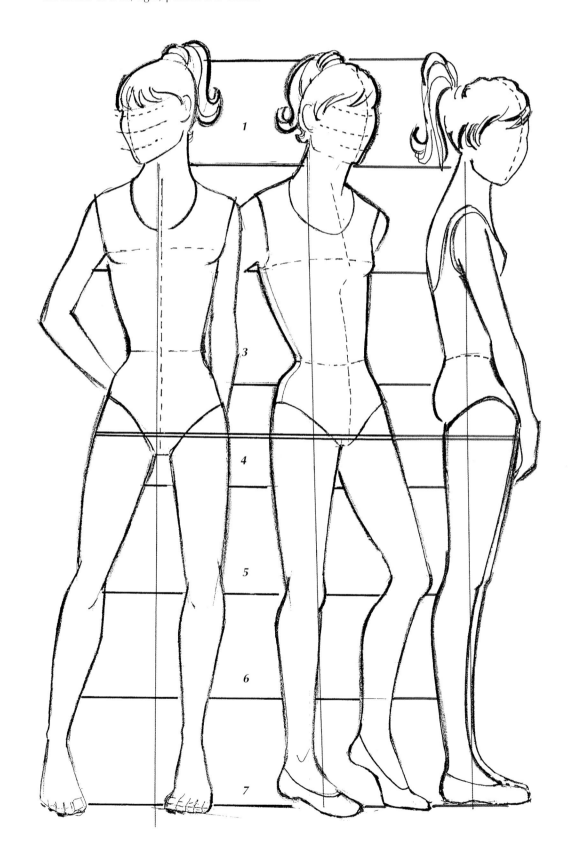

✔ Using more than one medium or technique in an illustration is effective provided that they work together to create a unified result. A combination of pencils, inks, marker pens, watercolours, pastels or crayons may be used. There are many techniques that can be used in one illustration.

Sketch book: Experiment with different techniques and media. When suggesting hairstyles it is effective to use a white wax crayon on the paper. A watercolour wash will resist the areas where the wax has been applied leaving areas of white as illustrated.

2B and 3B pencils, used for tonal effects on a textured cartridge paper

From one pose develop a number of poses viewing the figure from different angles. Note the balance lines from the pit of the neck to the foot to establish which leg is taking the weight of the figure. Note the angle of the shoulders and hips, also the centre front line indicating the contour of the figure

A free pencil sketch using a 4B pencil on a textured cartridge paper developed from the figure on the opposite page. The same pose has been used and reversed arranging the two figures together

Pen: Line drawing
The pen gives a clear line value. A variety of pens is available in different thicknesses of point. It is effective to use a combination of line values in the one drawing

Pencil: Tonal drawing
The pencil is a versatile drawing implement. Experiment with the different grades. An HB pencil for example gives a fine line value, in contrast a 2B or 3B is softer and ideal for shading and rendering tonal effects

Age Sixteen

Stage 1: *Figure pose developed from a photograph with a few simple lines to indicate the stance and attitude to use as a figure guide.*

Sketch produced with a soft 4B pencil for the finer details, a HB pencil was used emphasising the details of the drawing

Stage 2: *Design developed placing layout paper over the figures and drawing freely*

Stage 3: *For the effects of texture and tone - textured materials were placed under the paper and a wax crayon rubbed over the surface leaving areas of white suggesting light*

Presentation Board

Stage 4: Figures cut out leaving a margin of white paper round the figures mounted against the background. A small section of a photograph was enlarged on the photocopier to suggest the environment in which the design would be worn

Art Materials

A large selection of art materials is available. New items are constantly introduced, so offering you the opportunity to develop new techniques. Be aware of new products and experiment with them. Many art materials are available as single items as well as a complete range of colours. Initially, it is advisable to purchase a small selection of colours to discover how you relate to the medium. Often special papers, fixatives and solvents will be needed to achieve the required effects.

Fashion boards
High quality thick board that will take charcoal, crayon, gouache, tempera and watercolour paints.

Bristol board
The board has a high rag content with a fine white surface. Ideal for pen and ink work.

Pasteboard
An inexpensive white board for paste-up and general studio use.

Cartridge paper
White paper with a finely grained surface suitable for pencil, crayon and colour. This paper is made in different thicknesses and qualities.

Coloured cartridge paper
The surface has a slight texture. Suitable for colour work. Will take watercolour and pastels.

Layout pads
White layout detail paper with a surface ideal for ink and pencil. Available in different sizes.

Ingres paper
The surface of this paper is ideal for pastel and tempera work. Available in a good selection of colours.

Tracing paper and pads
Obtainable in sheets of different sizes or pads.

Detail paper
A white paper with a high degree of transparency. Suitable when working from original roughs.

Pencils (wood cased)
The degree of hardness is printed on each pencil:
6B is very soft, 9H very hard
F and HB medium
EX is extremely soft

Charcoal pencils
Give the same effect as pure charcoal sticks. Made in hard, medium or soft qualities.

Carbon pencils
This pencil will produce a dull matt finish.

Black pencils
Heavy extra large leads for bold drawings in matt jet black.

Coloured pencils
A large variety of makes is available with a good range of colours.

Watercolour pencils
Soft water soluble pencils. Use dry or wash over with a brush to achieve watercolour effects.

A large selection of pens is available; listed are some chosen for the different effects they achieve.

Rapidograph pens
Technical pens that provide a means of drawing without the need for constant refilling. The drawing point may be replaced with different sizes.

Technos drawing pen
The Pelikan Technos is a cartridge-filled drawing pen. Pen points are designed for different jobs, e.g. ruling, stencilling, and free hand. Many interchangeable points are available.

Marker pens
Large range of colours available. Quick drying. Chisel tip allows precise control of line from fine detail work to broad strokes. Obtainable with interchangable nibs in one barrel.

Osmiroid Sketch fountain pen
A very versatile sketching pen which provides a wide variety of line thickness from bold to a fine outline. This pen is fitted with a reservoir to maintain a constant ink flow. Indian ink should not be used.

Inks
Watercolour inks can be mixed with one another or diluted with water. A large range of colours is available. Very effective when used with the airbrush.

Acrylic colours
Extremely versatile, can be used with a variey of techniques. Easily diluted with water, but waterproof when dry.

A large selection of paints of varying qualities are manufactured:
Watercolours, Designer colours,
Coloured designer inks,
Tubes of oil paint.

Pastels
Pastels vary depending on the quality.

Coloured inks
A large selection of coloured inks are available, some of which are waterproof.

Brushes
Brushes are made in many sizes and qualities (sable, hog and squirrel hair).

Presentation books
Fitted with clear acetate pockets, ideal for the presentation of work.

Portfolios
Strong durable portfolios in different sizes for storing art work.

Leathercloth portfolios
Ideal for the protection and carrying of art work. Fitted with handle, two fasteners and a centre lock and key. Made in different sizes.

Cutting mats
Non-slip mats that provide a safe surface for all cutting jobs. Are printed with a grid. Special self-healing surface.

Protective sprays
Protect art work against damage. Obtainable in gloss or matt.

Spraymount
Remount creative adhesive allows you to lift and remount work without respraying. Allows experimentation with positioning of visuals prior to finished artwork.

Soft eraser
A white soft eraser for soft lead.

Light box
A box with a glass top containing a light, used for tracing.

Book List

Fashion Illustration

Barnes, Colin, *Fashion Illustration*, Macdonald, 1988
Boyes, Janet, *Essential Fashion Design*,
    Batsford, 1998
Drake, Nicholas, *Fashion Illustration*,
    Thames & Hudson, 1997, (Revised Edition)
Drake, Nicholas, *Fashion Illustration Today*,
    Thames & Hudson, 1987Macdonald, 1988
Ireland, Patrick John, *Fashion Design Illustration:
    Men*, Batsford, 1996
Ireland, Patrick John, *Fashion Design Illustration:
    Children*, Batsford, 1995
Ireland, Patrick John, *Fashion Design Illustration:
    Women*, Batsford, 1995
Ireland, Patrick John, *Fashion Graphics*, 1995
Ireland, Patrick John, *Introduction to Fashion
    Design*, 1995
Ireland, Patrick John, *Encyclopedia of
    Fashion Details*, Batsford, 1996
Ireland, Patrick John, *Fashion Design
    Drawing and Illustration*, Batsford, 1982
Ireland, Patrick John, *Introduction to Fashion
    Design*, Batsford, 1996
Seaman, Julian, *Professional Fashion Illustration*,
    Batsford, 1998
McKelvey, Kathryn, Janine Munslow,
    Illustrating Fashion, Blackwell Science,1997
McKelvey, Kathryn, *Fashion Source Book*,
    Blackwell Science, 1996
Parker, William, *Fashion Drawing in Vogue*,
    Thames & Hudson, 1983
Yajima, Isao, *Figure Drawing for Fashion*,
    Graphic-Sha, 1990

Graphics

The Artist's Manual, *Painting and Drawing Materials
    and Techniques*, Harper Collins, 1995
Cuthbert, Rosalind, *The Pastel Painter's Pocket
    Palette*, Batsford
Sidaway, Ian, *The Acrylic Painter's Pocket Palette*,
    Batsford, 1994
Smith, Ray, *The Artist Handbook*, Dorling
    Kindersley
Strother, Jane, *The Coloured Pencil Artist Pocket
    Palette*, Batsford
Welling, Richard, *Drawing with Markers*,
    Pitman, 1974

History of Fashion

The Fashion Book, Phaidon Press Ltd 1998.
De La Haye, Amy (Editor), *The Cutting Edge*,
    V & A 1997.
Rothstein, Natalie (Editor), *Four Hundred Years of Fashion*,
    Victoria and Albert Museum Publications, 1999
Bradfield, N., *Historical Costumes of England 1066-1968*
    Dobby, 1997
Knight, Margaret, *Fashion Through the Ages*,
    Tango Books 1998.
Tucker, Andrew, *The London Fashion Book*,
    Thames and Hudson 1998.
Steele, Valerie, *Women of Fashion, Twentieth
    Century Designers*, Rizzoli New York 1991.
O'Keefe, Linda, *Shoes*,
    Workman Publishing New York 1996.
Peacock, John, *20th Century Fashion*,
    Thames and Hudson 1998.
Peacock, John, *The Chronicle of Western Costume*,
    Thames and Hudson 1996.
Peacock, John, *Costume 1066-1990*,
    Thames and Hudson 1998.

Figure Drawing and Anatomy

Albert,Greg, *Basic Figure Drawing Techniques*
    Northlight Books, 1994
Constance,Diana, *An introduction to Drawing the
    Nude*, Apple, 1993
Coyle, Terence, *Master Class in Figure
    Drawing*, 1991
Gordon, Louise, *Anatomy and Figure Drawing*
    Batsford, 1996
Gordon, Louise, *The Figure in Action*
    Batsford, 1999
Barne Hogarth, *Dynamic Figure Drawing*, Watson
    Guptill, 1996
Hogarth, Barne, *Dynamic Figure Drawing*,
    Watson Guptill 1996
Könemass, *Anatomy Drawing School*, 1996
Loomis, Andrew, *Figure Drawing for all it's Worth*,
    Viking Press, 1971
Smith, Stan and Wheeler, Linda, *Drawing and
    Painting the Figure*, Phaidon, 1983

Index